FIRST AMERICANS
The Cree

RUTH BJORKLUND

 Marshall Cavendish
Benchmark
New York

For Olive and Arthur

ACKNOWLEDGMENTS

Series consultant: Raymond Bial

Marshall Cavendish
99 White Plains Road
Tarrytown, New York 10591-5502
www.marshallcavendish.us

Text, maps, and illustrations copyright © 2009 by Marshall Cavendish Corporation
Map and illustration by Rodica Prato
Craft illustrations by Chris Santoro

Library of Congress Cataloging-in-Publication Data
Bjorklund, Ruth.
The Cree / by Ruth Bjorklund.
p. cm. — (First Americans)
Summary: "Provides comprehensive information on the background, lifestyle,
beliefs, and present-day lives of the Cree people"—Provided by publisher.
Includes bibliographical references and index.
ISBN 978-0-7614-3020-9
1. Cree Indians—History—Juvenile literature.   2. Cree Indians—Social
life and customs—Juvenile literature.   I. Title.
E99.C88B59 2007
971.2004'973—dc22
2007035861

Front cover: A young Cree dancer dressed in ceremonial clothing
Title page: A painting of Chief Stone Child and Stone Child College, for whom the Cree-Chippewa reservation in Montana is named
Photo research by: Connie Gardner
Cover photo by Nativestock.com: Marilyn Angel Wynn
The photographs in this book are used by permission and through the courtesy of: *Nativestock.com:* Marilyn Angel Wynn: 1, 13, 18, 21, 25, 28, 36, 39; *North Wind Picture Archives:* 6, 16, 19; *Corbis:* Poodles Rock, 7; CORBIS, 15; Bettmann, 32; *Alamy:* Mary Evans Picture Library, 9; JTB Photo Communications, Inc., 23; Mega press, 33, 41; Bryan and Cherry Alexander Photography, 34; *The Image Works:* Mary Evans Picture Library, 10.

Editor: Deborah Grahame
Publisher: Michelle Bisson
Art Director: Anahid Hamparian
Series Designer: Symon Chow

Printed in Malaysia
1 3 5 6 4 2

CONTENTS

Hudson Bay

C R E E

James Bay

CANADA

UNITED STATES

MEXICO

N

0   300   600 mi

TRADITIONAL LANDS OF THE CREE

1 · A NORTHERN PEOPLE

Ancestors of the Cree have lived in Canada for more than 6,500 years. It is believed that they first settled along the shores of an icy clear bay, now known as James Bay, in eastern Canada. The people were hunters and gatherers who roamed the region, living on its bounty of roots, grasses, berries, animals, fish, and birds.

Over time the Cree formed several different bands, or tribal groups. Some lived along the eastern shore of James Bay in what is now the Canadian **province** of Quebec. Inland, west and south of Hudson's Bay, lived the Swampy Creek Cree. Further west lived the Western Woods or Woodland Cree. Later other bands formed and migrated to the western Plains or north to the Arctic Circle.

The Eastern bands lived in low-lying areas with lakes,

A map showing the hunting grounds of the Eastern Cree before Europeans arrived rivers, swamps, and ocean beaches. They fished and hunted big game animals such as caribou, moose, and black bear. They also trapped beavers, otters, lynx, and rabbits. The land was a rich habitat for birds and ducks. Some Cree hunted the icy coastal waters for beluga whales, fur seals, and polar bears. The Swampy Creek Cree lived near swamps and forests crisscrossed by rivers, creeks, and lakes. Moose and caribou and huge flocks of birds and water fowl thrived in the area. The Cree people lived in cone-shaped **tipis** and wooden

This woodcut etching shows Cree hunters pursuing a moose.

lodges, and paddled the waters in birch canoes. Although they were fortunate to live where plants and animals were plentiful, the Cree battled swarms of stinging insects in summer and bitter cold winds, snow, and ice in winter.

During one of these winters a crew of European explorers found their way to James Bay. In 1611 an Englishman named Henry Hudson piloted his ship across the North Atlantic and into a huge shallow bay in search of a route to the Pacific Ocean. Later he and his crew parted ways. Some historians

Adventurer Henry Hudson comes ashore during his third voyage to the New World.

believe that Hudson met a band of Cree and traded a few of his belongings for some beaver **pelts** to keep warm. No one really knows what happened to Hudson. But many other Europeans later followed his route and made their way to James Bay, changing the life of the Cree forever.

By the mid-1600s English and French adventurers were eagerly exploring North America. Many hoped to strike it rich by trapping beavers and selling the pelts in Europe. Beaver fur hats were a major fashion trend in Europe, where beavers had been hunted almost to **extinction**. The large bay that Henry Hudson had explored was now called Hudson's Bay. In 1670 the British king, Charles II, gave the land around Hudson's Bay and James Bay to European adventurers. The adventurers formed a trading business called Hudson's Bay Company. The Hudson's Bay Company traded with the Cree.

The Cree were friendly to the newcomers. They taught them survival skills and guided them through the bush, or wilderness. The European traders gave the Cree knives, metal

A Cree guide accompanies a European hunter as he stalks a herd of moose.

cooking pots, blankets, sewing needles, and other goods. In return the Cree trapped beaver pelts for the Europeans.

The Cree moved their homes and all their belongings from place to place in search of food. Because they did this they knew a great deal about the animals, the seasons, the best hunting grounds, and the other tribes in the region. When the Hudson's Bay Company and other Europeans built trading posts along the major trails and waterways, the Cree were regular visitors. Cree hunters trapped beaver and traded them at the posts for European goods. They also took European

Cree and French hunters meet to trade goods for pelts and hides.

goods into the bush to trade for pelts trapped by other tribes. The Cree were fond of European trade goods, such as knives, guns, and garments made out of cloth. Their desire for more of these goods sent the Cree farther away from James Bay, stretching their territory and making new trade agreements with tribes to the west and north.

As the Cree moved they met and married people from other tribes. Likewise many Cree women married English or French traders and trappers. Their children were known as Métis, which is a French word that means "mixed." These children grew up speaking French, English, and Cree. Because of the Cree's wide-ranging trade routes and intermarriages, Cree was the most common trade language spoken in Canada. The Cree became powerful traders and the richest tribe in the area.

However, by the middle of the 1700s, the Europeans were destroying the traditional life of the Cree. Many Cree began to live in villages close to the trading posts instead of moving about in small bands hunting for food. Because they lived near each other, and close to the English and French as well, disease spread easily among the Cree people. The Europeans carried disease-causing germs in their bodies that were often deadly to the native population. Entire villages were wiped out by smallpox, a painful disease carried by the Europeans.

Meanwhile it was getting harder for the Cree to survive. Due to overhunting, there were fewer beavers to trap, and the Europeans, especially the French, had learned how to do their own trapping. With fewer pelts, the Cree who depended on trade with the Hudson's Bay Company could no longer make a good living. Several bands of Cree chose to escape the sickness and the loss of their way of life by migrating west to the woodlands, prairies, and the Great Plains.

Wherever the Cree roamed, they quickly learned how to

live with their new surroundings. Out west the Cree began to follow **buffalo** herds. The earliest buffalo hunters on the Plains traveled on foot in small hunting parties. They forced the buffalo into pounds, fenced corrals made of logs. Once the hunters trapped their prey, they killed them with spears or bows and arrows.

By the time the Cree reached the Great Plains, buffalo hunting had changed. European explorers had taught Great Plains tribes to shoot guns and ride horses. The Cree had guns, but not horses. Sometimes they traded with other tribes for horses, but during the years 1810 to 1850, the Plains Cree and other tribes formed raiding parties and snuck into one another's camps at night to steal horses. Historians call this period the Horse Wars. Tribes teamed up and formed alliances, or friendships, to fight their enemies. The Plains Cree and the Ojibwe, or Chippewa, had an alliance. Their main enemy was the Blackfoot Nation.

On the Plains in the 1800s there were fewer buffalo

herds, and hunters often were caught **poaching** on one another's hunting grounds. In the late 1860s the Blackfoot and the Cree fought bitterly in several battles called the Buffalo Wars. Hundreds of Cree warriors were killed in one battle known as the Battle of Oldman River.

The Blackfoot and the Cree signed a peace treaty in 1871. But there would be no true peace for the Plains tribes. American and Canadian settlers moved into the region. They took over tribal land and killed off the buffalo herds. Many of

A Plains Cree horseman closes in on a buffalo in this Old West painting.

the non-Indian people killed buffalo for sport and left the animals' bodies to rot on the ground. This act of cruelty and wastefulness angered the tribes, and many warriors led attacks against the newcomers. But the Americans and Canadians built forts to protect their citizens and railroads to make it easier to move about the Plains. In the 1800s missionaries tried to convert the Cree to the Christian religion. Government officials outlawed many of the Cree's traditional religious **rituals**. They also took Cree children away from their families and sent them to boarding schools where they were punished for speaking their native language and forced to learn the ways of the settlers.

As settlers took over native lands, a Métis man named Louis Riel took a stand against them. Cree leaders joined him in the fight to stop the government from giving their land to white settlers. After a battle in 1885 called the North-West Rebellion, Riel and two Cree chiefs, Big Bear and Poundmaker, were captured. Fearing for the lives of their followers, Big Bear's son, Little Bear, guided a band of Cree south to Montana to live with the Chippewa tribe, led by Chief Stone Child. Later, in 1916, the U.S. government gave the Cree and Chippewa tribes a piece of land in Montana called a **reservation**. It was named Rocky Boy's Reservation after Chief Stone Child, whom the Americans had misnamed Chief Rocky Boy.

Today the Cree are Canada's largest native tribe. They live in cities and towns and also on many reservations (called reserves in Canada) throughout most of the country. Many of the Cree in the United States live in towns near the Canadian border. Rocky Boy's Reservation in Montana is the only Cree reservation in the United States, and it is shared with the Chippewa.

Métis activist Louis Riel was joined by Cree leaders in the North-West Rebellion.

2 · CLOSE TO NATURE

Once a small band of Cree living near James Bay was called Kenistenoag. The French fur traders called them Kristineaux, or Kri for short. The English spelled the name Cree. Most Cree call themselves the Nehiawak, which loosely means the true, or real, people.

From Canada's arctic north, across bays, swamps, and forests, to Montana's dry plains, the Cree lived close to nature. In fall they hunted big game such as moose, caribou, and bear. In winter they trapped otter and beaver, while in spring they hunted ducks, geese, and other birds. The Cree fished in summer and gathered roots, grasses, and berries. Arctic-dwelling Cree hunted whales, polar bear, caribou, and seals. In spring, summer, and fall they traveled on foot or by canoe,

Using a curved knife, a Cree canoe builder shapes the wooden frame before lashing on a birch bark skin.

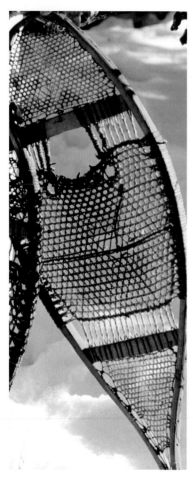

The Cree made many types of snowshoes to move about in different terrains.

which they built using carved wood and birch bark. To hunt in the snow the Cree wore snowshoes shaped like beaver tails, made of bent wood and string cut from animal skin. They also used dogsleds or toboggans (long wooden snow sleds). Plains Cree hunted on horseback for buffalo year-round and, when snow fell, they chased the buffalo into high snowdrifts.

Cree homes came from nature and changed with the seasons. In summer many Cree built tipis. These were cone-shaped dwellings typically crafted with fifteen poles, and covered in birch bark or animal skin. Each pole had a special meaning, such as respect, happiness, love, cleanliness, sharing, or hope. Fresh-smelling cedar boughs were placed on the floor. In winter tipis were wrapped in heavy animal hides such as caribou or elk. Some Woodland

In colder weather the Woodland Cree often covered their wigwams in caribou hide.

Cree built wigwams. These were dome-shaped houses covered in bark in summer. A thick layer of earth was added in winter. Usually only parents and their children lived together. Other Cree farther north and west built lodges in winter, and larger family groups lived in them. The lodges were rectangular buildings made of logs and sod. Two fires burned inside to keep everyone protected from the cold.

The turning of the seasons meant a change of clothing for the Cree. In summer many children under the age of five rarely wore clothing at all. Older children and adults wore light garments made of **buckskin**. Women and girls wore long dresses and buckskin leggings. They decorated these dresses with dyed porcupine quills, shells, and beads. Men wore a breechcloth, which is a simple, comfortable garment made of two flaps of buckskin belted around the waist. They also wore buckskin leggings and shirts. In winter they wore shirts made of beaver fur. Plains Cree wore similar garments made from elk or buffalo. Men and women wore beautiful buckskin shoes, called moccasins, which were covered with beadwork, embroidery, and fringe, and were sometimes lined with mosses or fur. In winter Cree men and women wore robes made of rabbit fur or moose hair. Plains Cree wore buffalo robes with the fur against their bodies for warmth.

Some fancy moccasins were made with decorated panels that could be removed and sewn onto a new pair of soles.

The Cree were artistic. They decorated their clothing with fancy sewing, feathers, beads, shells, and porcupine quills. The belts that Cree men and women wore were especially colorful. The Plains Cree carved designs in their buffalo robes and painted them with plant dyes and animal blood. Both men and women wore some jewelry, mostly hollow animal bones that they threaded into the braids of their hair, earrings, and necklaces made of beads, shells, or animal claws. Children had their ears pierced at an early age.

Cree women owned the family's tipi and could put it together in less than an hour. A man needed to ask his wife's permission to paint their home. Each Cree man had a guiding spirit,

A Cree man's dress coat, made of buckskin and decorated with beads and fringe

and he painted its image on the inside walls of his tipi to honor that spirit.

The European tools made some work easier, but old ways remained strong with the Cree. Women and men continued to perform traditional tasks. Women built the tipis or wigwams and took care of the children. They carried children on their backs in a **cradleboard**, something like a baby backpack. Women gathered fruits and berries and dug up roots, such as turnips. They also hunted small game such as rabbits and squirrels. They cooked and kept the camp and their homes clean. During summer when women picked berries, they made a special food called pemmican. Pemmican was something like a modern "power bar." It was made of dried meat mixed with berries and fat. Pemmican was healthy and an easy food to carry. It did not spoil and it helped keep people energized while they were on a hunt or during winter when there was little other food.

Cree women sewed clothing and tanned buckskin for fabric. Besides clothing Cree women made buckskin pouches and bags to carry important items such as knives, **herbs**, medicines, and sewing kits. Cree women also wove baskets from plants and buffalo hair, made bowls from clay, and carved cooking pots from soapstone.

Cree men were responsible for hunting for food. They made their tools, such as axes, knives, bows, arrows, traps, fishing nets, and poles. They also built canoes, toboggans, **travois**, and snowshoes. Woodcarvers made pipes, bowls, eating utensils, and hunting whistles. Artisans made rattles and drums to use in celebrations and ceremonies. Cree men had to know the seasons and the best

This buffalo meat, drying over an open fire, will be used to make pemmican.

hunting grounds and be skilled in making weapons. Most Plains Cree men were warriors. They were skilled horsemen

Nut Butter

Some of the most important foods that the Cree gathered in the woods were nuts and seeds. Women often made a delicious nut butter to spread on breads and other foods. To make your own nut butter you will need:

- 1 cup of nuts or seeds, such as walnuts, almonds, sesame, or mixed nuts
- 2 teaspoons honey or maple syrup
- Metal mixing bowl
- A rock about the size of your hand
- Mixing spoon

First wash the rock thoroughly with warm, soapy water and let it dry. Measure the nuts and pour them into the bowl. Use the rock to smash the nuts until they form a paste. Add honey or maple syrup and mix with a spoon. Spread on bread for a high-energy and delicious snack.

and brave fighters who defended their family and tribe. The best of these men were invited to join the Warrior Society, a group of important men who governed the tribe.

Boys spent their days with their fathers, uncles, and grandfathers. Girls learned from the female members of their family and tribe. But everyone came together to enjoy games, sports, storytelling, and festivals. Favorites among adults and children included games similar to hide-and-seek, football, lacrosse, tug-of-war, and guessing games. Children enjoyed toys such as **bull roarers**, rattles, whistles, toy bows and arrows, wooden dolls, and peashooters. Children brought great joy to their families and were deeply loved.

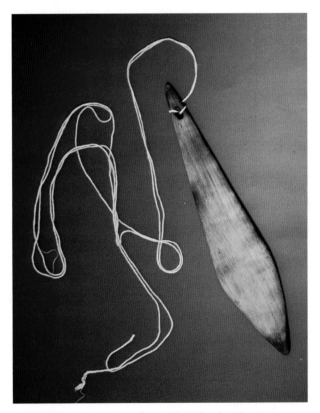

This bull roarer makes a loud, rhythmic roar when swung by its string.

Cup and Pin Game

Traditional Cree children's toys were a fun way to learn adult life skills. The cup and pin game helped them improve hand-to-eye coordination to prepare Cree children for hunting and trapping small animals and fish. To play the game the Cree used a bone needle, a piece of leather, a leather string, and several hollow animal bones.

You will need:

- An index card, or a piece of cardboard, about 4x6 inches (10 cm x 15 cm)
- A sturdy length of string about 18 inches (46 centimeters) long
- 1 empty toilet paper roll
- Crayons, markers, or paint (if you wish)
- Scissors
- An unsharpened pencil
- Hole punch

To make your game punch 6 holes, all equally spaced around the index card, plus one extra hole at one end, to tie the string onto. Tie one end of the string to the seventh hole. Be sure to punch the other 6 holes large enough so that the pencil will be able to poke through.

Color or paint the toilet paper roll, if you wish. Then cut the toilet paper roll into 6 cardboard rings. Thread each ring onto the cord. Then tie the loose end of the cord to the eraser end of the pencil. Players decide how many points will end the game, such as a minimum of 12, or a long game of 100. Generally, players earn 1 point for catching each cardboard ring, extra points, (such as 2–10) for catching the cardboard ring closest to the pencil (more difficult) and if they catch the index card, a point for each hole on the index card.

How to Play:

Hold the pencil, eraser side down, in one hand away from you. In the other hand, hold the index card against you. Be sure the string is straight and tight. When ready, toss the index card up and away from you. With the pencil, try to catch as many cardboard rings, or the index card end, as you can. If you miss, you pass the game on to the next player. If you score, you keep playing until you miss. The first player to reach the agreed winning score wins.

Keep score with paper and pencil or if you are outside, do it as the Cree did, with hash marks made in the dirt with a stick!

3 · SACRED BELIEFS

The Cree believe that spirits live inside everything on the earth. The Cree respect the natural world and honor the spirits of the four winds, the sun, moon, and stars, and the rivers, bays, lakes, swamps, plains, and forests. They pay tribute to the spirits in all the fishes, birds, animals, and plants. When hunters track and kill prey, they first honor the animal's spirit with a greeting and a prayer. When picking berries, gathering herbs, or chopping wood, a Cree sends a message of thanks to the spirits. The Cree believe they have a spirit inside their bodies. It comes to them when they are born and leaves when they die. The spirits then rise up beyond the stars to a place they call Oskaskog-Wask, meaning the "Green Grass World."

The sun sets over a horse pasture in Rocky Boy's Reservation.

The Cree believe in a creator, or Great Spirit, whom they call **Kitchi-Kitchi Manito** (Great, Great Spirit). He lives within all living things and helps the Cree find food, shelter, and good fortune. He also protects the Cree from evil spirits. The most terrifying is called **Matchi-Manito** (Evil Spirit). He brings disease, hardship, and sorrow to the people. He lives inside dangerous plants and animals, such as thorn bushes, snakes, and mountain lions. Other evil spirits were giants called Windigos who chased down humans and ate them. The Cree also believed in a trickster spirit called Wisakedjak. In English this trickster was called Whiskey Jack. The Cree saw Whiskey Jack as a powerful spirit, sometimes good and sometimes frightening. Whiskey Jack's power came from cheating and joking. It was wise to be wary of him.

Because spirits lived all around them the Cree sought help and guidance from a holy person, called a shaman. A Cree shaman could be either a man or a woman. Shamans had special powers and the ability to understand and communicate with certain spirits. Some shamans were healers who provided medicines and asked the spirits for a cure. Some were believed to have magical powers. Other shamans forecasted the future. The Cree still practice these rituals with shamans along with their Christian beliefs.

Many Cree carried small animal skin pouches filled with herbs and special medicines for health and good luck.

The Cree held ceremonies for a variety of reasons. Many of their celebrations offered prayers for a successful hunt or gave thanks for one. People also came together to sing, dance, and chant before going to war. Later they celebrated winning with a war dance. The Sun Dance was the most sacred ceremony for the Plains Cree. Each year around the first day of summer the people gathered for several days to honor their creator, Kitchi-Kitchi Manito. They prayed and gave thanks and asked the creator to cure the sick and ease suffering. Young men pierced their bodies and young women wore their best finery. Key tribal members built a special tent for the Sun Dance. People made peace with each other and danced, sang, feasted, and honored the many gifts of the buffalo.

A young Cree man displays his bravery during the Sun Dance ceremony.

One of the most important rituals for a Cree tribal member happened early in life. It was called the Walking-Out ceremony, and it is still practiced to this day. The ceremony is performed for each child once the child has learned to walk. Elders and other tribal members come together in a large tent. In another tent families prepare the young children. Parents dress the children in traditional clothing made of beads and animal hide. They spread tree branches to form a path from one tent, across the camp, toward the other tent. The children carry small sacks of food to offer to the elders. They also carry toy tools. Little boys carry toy bows and arrows or hunting rifles. Girls carry toy axes, shovels, or cooking utensils. With the help of their mothers the children leave the tent and walk along the path, stopping by the woodpile. There boys practice hunting with their toy weapons and girls practice chopping wood with their toy axes. Then they enter the tent where the

A Cree toddler is dressed in finery and greeted at the Walking-Out ceremony.

rest of the tribe is waiting and offer their sacks of food. The elders kiss them and welcome them into Cree society. A great feast follows.

4 · THE CREE TODAY

Today more than 200,000 people are members of the Cree tribe, and more than 100,000 are Métis, with Cree heritage. The Cree and Métis live a modern life that is made richer by honoring and preserving Cree tradition.

Cree reserves in Canada are scattered across the country. Some are near cities, and others are in the wilderness. In the United States there is only one reservation, the Chippewa-Cree Rocky Boy's Reservation, 50 miles (80 kilometers) south of the border with Canada. The reservation was first created in 1916 and was made larger in 1947. Today the reservation has 122,000 acres (49,373 hectares) of rolling plains, grasslands, alpine forests, and hills. The hills, known as the Bear's Paw Mountains, have a small ski area and are near Beaver Creek Park, the largest county park in the United States.

Canoes and a traditional tipi stand in the backyard of a present-day Cree home.

Rocky Boy's Reservation and the many reserves in Canada are each led by a tribal chief and **council**. The chief can be a man or a woman, and all the council members are elected by the people. One of the most important roles of the tribal government is to communicate the needs and the rights of the Cree people to the governments of Canada and the United States. Many tribes have natural resources that the govern-

The Bear's Paw Mountains lie at the western edge of Rocky Boy's Reservation, home to a county park and a ski area.

ments want. Some have oil on their land, others have trees for logging, and others have water that can be dammed and used to produce electric power. For many years the chiefs and their tribal governments have asked the U.S. and Canadian governments to respect their rights. One band settled a large claim with the Canadian government over plans to dam part of James Bay. Another Canadian band is still protesting oil wells in the area that pollute their community. In Montana the tribal council of Rocky Boy's Reservation has been working steadily to improve living conditions for the people. In deals made with the state of Montana and the U.S. government, the tribe has built a new vocational school and a large, modern health-care clinic, and has signed an agreement that provides a better water supply for drinking and for farming.

The Cree make their living in many different ways. Those who live in urban areas have more opportunity for jobs that pay well, such as careers in engineering, medicine, or commercial mining, logging, and fishing. Those who live in rural areas have a harder time earning a living.

Rocky Boy's Powwow

Every year since the first weekend in August 1964, the residents of Rocky Boy's Reservation have hosted a powwow. Dancers, singers, drummers, and tribal leaders are featured at the powwow. The performers wear elaborate outfits called **regalia** made of buckskin, fringe, beads, feathers, and religious objects. There are many types of dances, such as the Fancy Dance and the Grass Dance. Men, women, and children compete for prizes and honor. The Traditional Dance performed by Plains Cree men copies the movements of birds, buffalo, and other animals. Other dancers act out a successful hunt. The best dancers always keep the fringe on their clothing in motion. A musical women's dance is the Jingle Dress Dance. It was once performed to help heal the sick. The dancer wears tin cones tied to her dress. Some dancers wear one cone for each day of the year.

Grass Dancers get ready to perform at a Rocky Boy's Reservation powwow.

Food and supplies cost more and there are fewer jobs in these rural areas. Most of the people with jobs work for the tribe managing natural resources, teaching in schools, or working for the tribal police, fire department, and other community services. Families without jobs are usually very poor and often must rely on government payments. There are many Cree who prefer the old ways and continue to hunt, fish, and trap. Some make and use their own tools, while others use modern tools such as gasoline motors on their boats, woodworking machinery, and steel traps. The Canadian government passed a law in the early 1990s that promised to pay those Cree who hunt, trap, and fish to feed their families and their communities.

Cree craftsmanship remains an important part of their culture. Talented craftspeople earn a living making and selling traditional clothing to tribal members to wear for ceremonies and special occasions. Others earn a little extra money selling handmade moccasins, snowshoes, baskets, beadwork, and wooden toys to tourists.

Most Cree communities, urban or rural, have many

Students in many Cree communities often speak and write in the Cree language better than their parents.

modern conveniences in their homes, such as electricity and running water, as well as satellite TV, computers, the Internet, and cell phones. Those living in or near cities also benefit from quality health care. Many of the schools, especially those in rural areas, teach students their native Cree language, both spoken and written. Rocky Boy's Reservation is also the home of Stone Child College, a community college established in 1984. Through the efforts of the Cree people, their language and culture remains strong today, and although there have been challenges, the Cree take enormous pride in their heritage.

· TIME LINE

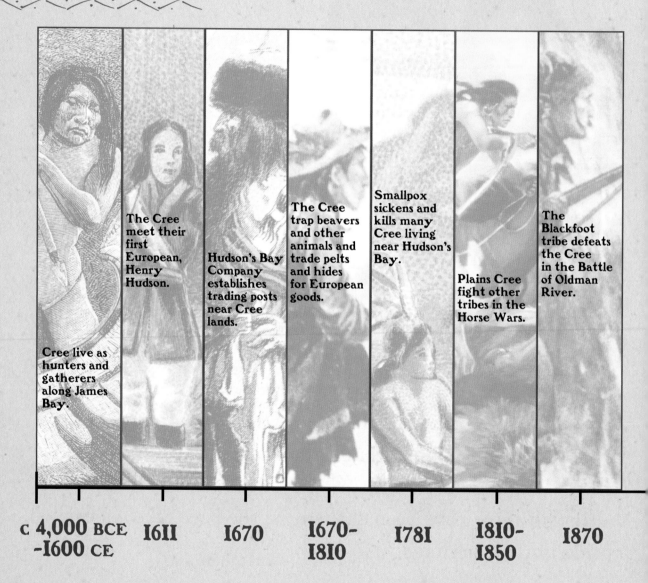

Cree live as hunters and gatherers along James Bay.

The Cree meet their first European, Henry Hudson.

Hudson's Bay Company establishes trading posts near Cree lands.

The Cree trap beavers and other animals and trade pelts and hides for European goods.

Smallpox sickens and kills many Cree living near Hudson's Bay.

Plains Cree fight other tribes in the Horse Wars.

The Blackfoot tribe defeats the Cree in the Battle of Oldman River.

c 4,000 BCE -1600 CE

1611

1670

1670- 1810

1781

1810- 1850

1870

Louis Riel and Cree chiefs Poundmaker and Big Bear are captured in the North-West Rebellion.

Rocky Boy's Reservation is created by the U.S. government.

Rocky Boy's Reservation hosts its first powwow.

Stone Child Community College is established.

U.S. President Bill Clinton signs a bill granting water rights from Lake Elwell to the Chippewa-Cree tribe.

A new, modern medical center opens on Rocky Boy's Reservation.

1885

1916

1964

1984

1999

2007

· GLOSSARY

buckskin: Strong, soft leather made from the skins of deer or sheep.

buffalo: A word used in North America to refer to the bison, the largest animal on the continent.

bull roarers: Wooden toys that make a whizzing sound when swung.

council: A group of people who are elected to govern.

cradleboard: A wooden board partially covered with hide that a mother used to carry her baby.

extinction: The killing off of all members of a species.

herbs: Plants used for healing, cooking, or religious ceremonies.

Kitchi-Kitchi Manito: The Cree great spirit and creator.

Matchi-Manito: The Cree evil spirit.

pelt: The skin and fur removed from an animal.

poaching: Entering another's land without permission to hunt and steal wild game.

province: A region of Canada that is like a U.S. state.

regalia: Special clothing worn at powwows and other ceremonies.

reservation: An area of land set aside by the U.S. government for a Native American tribe or nation.

rituals: Ceremonial acts or actions.

tipis: The tentlike houses of the Cree and other Great Plains tribes. Also spelled *teepee*.

travois: A dog- or horse-drawn sledlike device used to haul heavy loads.

· FIND OUT MORE

Books

Auger, Dale. *Mwakwa—Talks to the Loon: A Cree Story for Children.* Victoria, BC: Heritage House, 2006.

Bial, Raymond. *The Cree.* New York: Marshall Cavendish, 2005.

Ryan, Marla Felkins, and Linda Schmittroth, eds. *Cree.* San Diego: Blackbirch Press, 2003.

Stout, Mary. *Cree.* Milwaukee, WI: Gareth Stevens, 2004.

Web Sites

Cree Indian Fact Sheet
http//:www.geocities.com/bigorrin/cree_kids.htm

Cree Nation of Wemindji
http//:www.wemindji-nation.qc.ca

Cree Snowshoe Making
http//:www.birchbarkcanoe.net/snowshoes-beavertail.htm

About the Author
Ruth Bjorklund lives on Bainbridge Island near Seattle, Washington, with her husband, two children, four dogs, and a cat. Her grandfather was French Canadian and from him she inherited a love for paddling and fishing in cold, northern lakes.

· INDEX

Page numbers in **boldface** are illustrations.